MW01131627

MATH

FRACTIONS & DECIMALS

Eric Charlesworth

To O-we-o for being an outstanding meerkat.—E. C.

Editor: Sarah Longhi
Cover designer: Jason Robinson
Interior designer: Kelli Thompson
Illustrator: Teresa Anderko

ISBN-13: 978-0-545-15044-6
ISBN-10: 0-545-15044-2

1 2 3 4 5 6 7 8 9 10   40   16 15 14 13 12 11 10

New York • Toronto • London • Auckland • Sydney **Teaching** *Resources*
Mexico City • New Delhi • Hong Kong • Buenos Aires

Contents

Introduction

For students in grades 3 to 6, understanding the concept of the partial number (fractions, decimals, and percentages) is at the forefront of the math curriculum. Though it is listed under the NCTM strand of Numbers and Operations, a facility with fractions and their other representations supports students' understanding of geometry, measurement, probability, and the more complex algebra work that they are just beginning to undertake.

This book is designed to reinforce the conceptual understanding of non-whole numbers. The activities cover 16 key skills that progress from basic (finding equivalent fractions) to complex (converting fractions to percents). By using Sudoku puzzles to frame the problems, practicing these important skills becomes more fun and far more rewarding.

You can replace most rote facts-practice worksheets with the 41 leveled Sudoku puzzle challenges in this collection. A key advantage to using these puzzles is that the puzzles are self-checking. If students make an error, they will quickly find that the puzzle isn't working, which will help them catch the mistake and try to correct it themselves.

How to Use This Book

These puzzles can be used flexibly. You may want to hand out copies of the puzzles for a warm-up activity (or "do now") to start class. However, they can also be given to students who finish their class work early or occasionally serve as homework.

Have students who are ready for a challenge solve the Word Problems that appear at the bottom of some of the puzzle pages. You may also invite them to use a 4-by-4 grid to create their own Sudoku puzzle for their peers.

Students who are struggling can use the Skills Reference Sheet (pages 5 and 6) to help them remember basic concepts. Be sure to model specific skills for individual students or solve puzzles on the overhead or the interactive whiteboard for the class. The tips included at the bottom of some of the Sudoku puzzle pages may also provide helpful hints about the target skill.

$\frac{2}{4} = \frac{}{2}$	$\frac{12}{16} = \frac{3}{}$	$\frac{2}{6} = \frac{1}{}$	$\frac{4}{8} = \frac{}{4}$
$\frac{6}{9} = \frac{}{3}$	$\frac{1}{10} = \frac{}{30}$	$\frac{1}{1} = \frac{4}{}$	$\frac{3}{24} = \frac{}{8}$
$\frac{1}{2} = \frac{}{8}$	$\frac{3}{9} = \frac{}{3}$	$\frac{4}{10} = \frac{}{5}$	$\frac{2}{2} = \frac{}{3}$
$\frac{9}{15} = \frac{}{5}$	$\frac{1}{4} = \frac{}{8}$	$\frac{10}{10} = \frac{}{1}$	$\frac{8}{10} = \frac{}{5}$

✳ NCTM Standard Connection

The student will
- make equivalent fractions
- simplify fractions
- convert improper fractions to mixed numbers and fractions to decimals
- add, subtract, multiply, and divide fractions and decimals
- use fractions and decimals to solve word problems

Super SUDOKU RULES

Rule 1

▶ Fill the **row** so that it contains numbers 1 through 4.

1	2	3	4
3	4	1	2
2	1	4	3
4	3	2	1

Rule 2

▶ Fill the **column** so that it contains numbers 1 through 4.

1	2	3	4
3	4	1	2
2	1	4	3
4	3	2	1

Rule 3

▶ Fill the 2-by-2 **box** so that it contains numbers 1 through 4.

1	2	3	4
3	4	1	2
2	1	4	3
4	3	2	1

Notes

For some of the 4-by-4 puzzles in this book, you will fill in the spaces with 1, 2, 3, and 4. Other puzzles may ask you to use a different set of numbers, such as 5, 6, 7, and 8.

Super Sudoku Math: Fractions & Decimals • © 2010 by Eric Charlesworth • Scholastic Teaching Resources

Skills Reference Sheet

Naming Fractions

Denominator = how many equal parts the object is divided into

Numerator = how many parts you have

Example: $\square\square\square\square\square = \frac{3}{5}$

Making Equivalent Fractions

Multiply (or divide) both the denominator and numerator by the same number.

Example: Find two fractions that are equivalent to $\frac{1}{2}$.

Answer: $\frac{1}{2} \times \frac{2}{2} = \frac{2}{4} \times \frac{2}{2} = \frac{4}{8}$

$\frac{1}{2} = \frac{2}{4} = \frac{4}{8}$

Simplifying Fractions

1. Find the greatest common factor (GCF) of the numerator and denominator.

2. Divide both parts of that fraction by the GCF.

Example: Put $\frac{12}{30}$ in simplest form.

Answer: Greatest common factor = 6

$\frac{12}{30} \div \frac{6}{6} = \frac{2}{5}$

Mixed Numbers and Improper Fractions

Fractions that are greater than a whole can be written two ways.

Example:

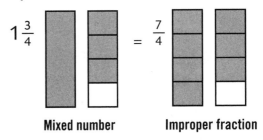

Mixed number   Improper fraction

Adding and Subtracting Fractions

1. Convert the fractions so they have the same denominator.

2. Complete the operation.

Example: $\frac{5}{8} + \frac{1}{4}$

Answer: $\frac{1}{4} \times \frac{2}{2} = \frac{2}{8}$ $\frac{5}{8} + \frac{2}{8} = \frac{7}{8}$

Multiplying Fractions

Multiply across both numerators and denominators.

Example: $\frac{2}{3} \times \frac{4}{5} = \frac{8}{15}$

Dividing Fractions

1. Flip the divisor fraction.

2. Multiply across.

Example: $\frac{1}{4} \div \frac{3}{5}$

1. Flip $\frac{3}{5}$ so it becomes $\frac{5}{3}$.

2. Multiply: $\frac{1}{4} \times \frac{5}{3} = \frac{5}{12}$

Super

SUDOKU

Skills Reference Sheet

Finding the Fraction of a Whole

1. Multiply the whole number by the numerator.

2. Divide by the denominator.

Example: What is $\frac{2}{3}$ of 60?

Answer: First multiply: $60 \times 2 = 120$.
Then divide: $120 \div 3 = 40$.

Converting Fractions to Decimals

1. Convert to an equivalent fraction with a denominator to a power of ten.

2. Write the fraction as a decimal.

Examples: $\frac{4}{5} \times \frac{2}{2} = \frac{8}{10} = 0.8$

$\frac{7}{20} \times \frac{5}{5} = \frac{35}{100} = 0.35$

Some Common Fraction-Decimal Equivalents

Fraction	Decimal
$\frac{3}{4}$	0.75
$\frac{1}{2}$	0.5
$\frac{2}{5}$	0.4
$\frac{1}{4}$	0.25
$\frac{1}{5}$	0.2
$\frac{1}{10}$	0.1

Adding and Subtracting Decimals

1. Line up your decimal points.
2. Add zeroes to hold place values, if needed.
3. Complete the operation.

Example:

$$2.3 + 2.41 \qquad 7.65 - 4.2$$

$$\begin{array}{r} 2.30 \\ +\ 2.41 \\ \hline 4.71 \end{array} \qquad \begin{array}{r} 7.65 \\ -\ 4.20 \\ \hline 3.45 \end{array}$$

Multiplying Decimals

1. Count the number of digits after the decimal point in each factor

2. Count that same number of digits from the right in your product. Mark the decimal point at that place.

Example: 3.77×2.8

$$\begin{array}{r} 3.77 \quad \text{(2 decimal places)} \\ \times \quad 2.8 \quad \text{(1 decimal place)} \\ \hline 3016 \\ +\ 7540 \\ \hline 10.556 \quad \text{(3 decimal places)} \end{array}$$

Converting Fractions to Percents

Convert the denominator to 100.

Example: $\frac{7}{10} \times \frac{10}{10} = \frac{70}{100} = 70\%$

Finding the Percent of a Number

1. Convert the percent to a decimal.
2. Multiply that decimal by the number.

Example: What is 75% of 40?

$$75\% = \frac{75}{100} = .75$$

$$40 \times .75 = 30$$

Super Sudoku Math: Fractions & Decimals • © 2010 by Eric Charlesworth • Scholastic Teaching Resources

6

Name _____ Date _____

Naming Fractions

Directions

● Every row, column, and 2-by-2 box  should contain each of these digits:

1 2 3 4

● Fill in each blank with the correct number to name the fraction.

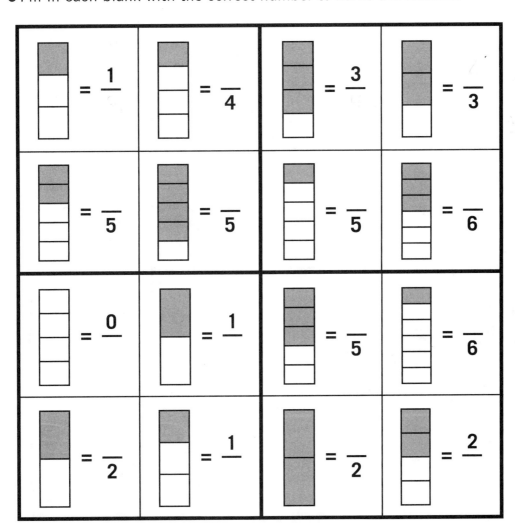

Tip!

When your numerator gets larger, your value is larger because you have more shaded pieces. But when your denominator gets larger your value is smaller because the shaded pieces are smaller in size.

Super SUDOKU

Name _____ Date _____

Naming Fractions

Directions

● Every row, column, and 2-by-2 box ⊞ should contain each of these digits:

4 **5** **6** **7**

● Fill in each blank with the correct number to name the fraction.

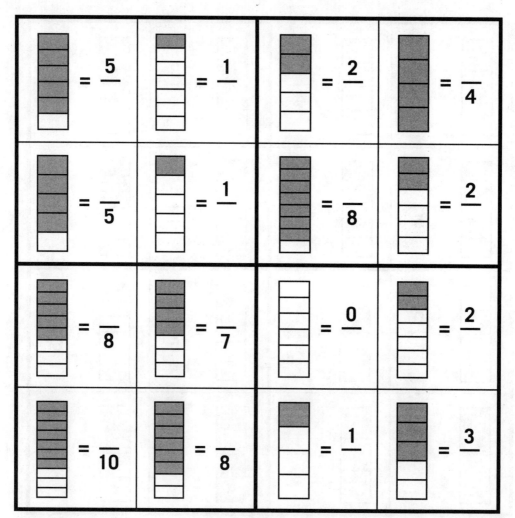

Tip!

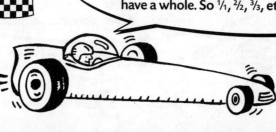

Anytime your denominator and numerator are the same number, you have every piece shaded in. That means you have a whole. So ⅟₁, ²⁄₂, ³⁄₃, etc. are all equal to one!

8

Super Sudoku Math: Fractions & Decimals • © 2010 by Eric Charlesworth • Scholastic Teaching Resources

Super SUDOKU

Name _____ Date _____

Making Equivalent Fractions

Directions

● Every row, column, and 2-by-2 box should contain each of these digits:

1 2 3 4

● Fill in each blank with the correct number to create a pair of equivalent fractions.

$\dfrac{2}{4} = \dfrac{1}{2}$	$\dfrac{12}{16} = \dfrac{3}{4}$	$\dfrac{2}{6} = \dfrac{1}{\_}$	$\dfrac{4}{8} = \dfrac{\_}{4}$
$\dfrac{6}{9} = \dfrac{2}{3}$	$\dfrac{1}{10} = \dfrac{3}{30}$	$\dfrac{1}{1} = \dfrac{4}{\_}$	$\dfrac{3}{24} = \dfrac{\_}{8}$
$\dfrac{1}{2} = \dfrac{\_}{8}$	$\dfrac{3}{9} = \dfrac{\_}{3}$	$\dfrac{4}{10} = \dfrac{\_}{5}$	$\dfrac{2}{2} = \dfrac{\_}{3}$
$\dfrac{9}{15} = \dfrac{\_}{5}$	$\dfrac{1}{4} = \dfrac{\_}{8}$	$\dfrac{10}{10} = \dfrac{\_}{1}$	$\dfrac{8}{10} = \dfrac{\_}{5}$

Tip!

Equivalent fractions like ½ and ²⁄₄ have the same value, but they're broken into different size pieces. So instead of getting one piece of a cake that has been split in half, you get two smaller pieces of a cake that has been split in fourths. Same tasty cake, just more plates!

Super SUDOKU

Name _____ Date _____

Making Equivalent Fractions

Directions

● Every row, column, and 2-by-2 box ⊞ should contain each of these digits:

6 7 8 9

● Fill in each blank with the correct number to create a pair of equivalent fractions.

$\dfrac{2}{14} = \dfrac{1}{\underline{}}$	$\dfrac{1}{2} = \dfrac{4}{\underline{}}$	$\dfrac{2}{3} = \dfrac{6}{\underline{}}$	$\dfrac{1}{4} = \dfrac{\underline{}}{24}$
$\dfrac{2}{3} = \dfrac{\underline{}}{9}$	$\dfrac{1}{3} = \dfrac{\underline{}}{27}$	$\dfrac{4}{14} = \dfrac{2}{\underline{}}$	$\dfrac{2}{16} = \dfrac{1}{\underline{}}$
$\dfrac{6}{16} = \dfrac{3}{\underline{}}$	$\dfrac{1}{4} = \dfrac{\underline{}}{28}$	$\dfrac{2}{3} = \dfrac{4}{\underline{}}$	$\dfrac{1}{3} = \dfrac{3}{\underline{}}$
$\dfrac{1}{2} = \dfrac{\underline{}}{18}$	$\dfrac{10}{12} = \dfrac{5}{\underline{}}$	$\dfrac{3}{4} = \dfrac{6}{\underline{}}$	$\dfrac{1}{2} = \dfrac{\underline{}}{14}$

Word Problem

Steven just finished his basketball game in which he made 10 out of 15 shots. Can you think of more than one way to say what fraction of shots he made?

_____

Super Sudoku Math: Fractions & Decimals • © 2010 by Eric Charlesworth • Scholastic Teaching Resources

Super SUDOKU

Name _____ Date _____

Mixed Review 1
(Naming Fractions and Making Equivalent Fractions)

Directions

• Every row, column, and 2-by-2 box ⊞ should contain each of these digits:

1 **2** **3** **4**

• Fill in each blank with the correct number.

$= \dfrac{1}{}$	$\dfrac{5}{10} = \dfrac{1}{}$	$= \dfrac{}{6}$	$\dfrac{2}{16} = \dfrac{}{8}$
$\dfrac{30}{40} = \dfrac{}{4}$	$= \dfrac{}{3}$	$\dfrac{1}{4} = \dfrac{}{16}$	$= \dfrac{}{5}$
$\dfrac{7}{7} = \dfrac{1}{}$	$= \dfrac{3}{}$	$\dfrac{4}{14} = \dfrac{}{7}$	$\dfrac{1}{7} = \dfrac{}{21}$
$\dfrac{8}{16} = \dfrac{}{4}$	$\dfrac{6}{20} = \dfrac{}{10}$	$\dfrac{50}{100} = \dfrac{}{2}$	$= \dfrac{4}{}$

Tip!

Any time the numerator is half of the denominator (example: $^6/_{12}$), that fraction can be simplified to ½. Any time the numerator is one-third of the denominator (example: $^3/_9$), that fraction can be simplified to ⅓. Yes, it works for simplifying to ¼, ⅕, ⅙, and all the rest, too!

Super SUDOKU

Name _____ Date _____

Simplifying Fractions

Directions

● Every row, column, and 2-by-2 box ⊞ should contain each of these digits:

1   2   3   4

● Fill in each blank with correct number to show the fraction in its simplest form.

$\dfrac{4}{18} = \dfrac{}{9}$	$\dfrac{6}{18} = \dfrac{1}{}$	$\dfrac{8}{14} = \dfrac{}{7}$	$\dfrac{3}{27} = \dfrac{}{9}$
$\dfrac{20}{40} = \dfrac{}{2}$	$\dfrac{5}{20} = \dfrac{1}{}$	$\dfrac{6}{15} = \dfrac{}{5}$	$\dfrac{6}{8} = \dfrac{}{4}$
$\dfrac{6}{14} = \dfrac{}{7}$	$\dfrac{20}{30} = \dfrac{}{3}$	$\dfrac{5}{25} = \dfrac{}{5}$	$\dfrac{9}{12} = \dfrac{3}{}$
$\dfrac{8}{18} = \dfrac{}{9}$	$\dfrac{8}{80} = \dfrac{}{10}$	$\dfrac{9}{27} = \dfrac{1}{}$	$\dfrac{6}{12} = \dfrac{1}{}$

Tip!

You put a fraction in simplest terms by dividing both the numerator and denominator by the greatest common factor (GCF) of the numbers.

Super Sudoku Math: Fractions & Decimals • © 2010 by Eric Charlesworth • Scholastic Teaching Resources

Super SUDOKU

Super Sudoku Math: Fractions & Decimals • © 2010 by Eric Charlesworth • Scholastic Teaching Resources

Name _____ Date _____

Simplifying Fractions

Directions

● Every row, column, and 2-by-2 box ⊞ should contain each of these digits:

4 5 6 7

● Fill in each blank with correct number to show the fraction in its simplest form.

$\dfrac{8}{22} = \dfrac{\ }{11}$	$\dfrac{25}{30} = \dfrac{5}{\ }$	$\dfrac{21}{24} = \dfrac{\ }{8}$	$\dfrac{3}{15} = \dfrac{1}{\ }$
$\dfrac{14}{35} = \dfrac{2}{\ }$	$\dfrac{14}{20} = \dfrac{\ }{10}$	$\dfrac{25}{100} = \dfrac{1}{\ }$	$\dfrac{4}{24} = \dfrac{1}{\ }$
$\dfrac{60}{70} = \dfrac{\ }{7}$	$\dfrac{75}{100} = \dfrac{3}{\ }$	$\dfrac{30}{42} = \dfrac{\ }{7}$	$\dfrac{12}{28} = \dfrac{3}{\ }$
$\dfrac{22}{77} = \dfrac{2}{\ }$	$\dfrac{20}{100} = \dfrac{1}{\ }$	$\dfrac{2}{12} = \dfrac{1}{\ }$	$\dfrac{24}{30} = \dfrac{\ }{5}$

Word Problem

Lisa says she can play ⅔ of the songs that are in her piano book. Gina says she can play ⁴⁄₆ of the songs in the same book. Who can play more songs?

_____

Super SUDOKU

Name _____ Date _____

Converting Mixed Numbers & Improper Fractions

Directions

● Every row, column, and 2-by-2 box ⊞ should contain each of these digits:

6   7   8   9

● Fill in each blank with correct number to convert the mixed number to an improper fraction.

$4\frac{1}{2} = \frac{\ }{2}$	$3\frac{1}{7} = \frac{22}{\ }$	$2\frac{2}{3} = \frac{\ }{3}$	$1\frac{1}{5} = \frac{\ }{5}$
$1\frac{5}{6} = \frac{11}{\ }$	$1\frac{3}{5} = \frac{\ }{5}$	$2\frac{1}{4} = \frac{\ }{4}$	$1\frac{1}{6} = \frac{\ }{6}$
$2\frac{1}{8} = \frac{17}{\ }$	$1\frac{2}{4} = \frac{\ }{4}$	$2\frac{1}{3} = \frac{\ }{3}$	$1\frac{1}{9} = \frac{10}{\ }$
$1\frac{2}{5} = \frac{\ }{5}$	$1\frac{4}{5} = \frac{\ }{5}$	$5\frac{1}{6} = \frac{31}{\ }$	$1\frac{1}{7} = \frac{\ }{7}$

Tip!

When you convert from mixed numbers to improper fractions and vice-versa, your denominator should never change! For example $\frac{9}{5} = 1\frac{4}{5}$ because you're not changing the size of the pieces, you are just accounting for the number of the pieces.

Super Sudoku Math: Fractions & Decimals • © 2010 by Eric Charlesworth • Scholastic Teaching Resources

Super SUDOKU

Name _____ Date _____

Converting Mixed Numbers & Improper Fractions

Directions

- Every row, column, and 2-by-2 box ⊞ should contain each of these digits:

  1   **2**   **3**   **4**

- Fill in each blank with correct number to convert the improper fraction to a mixed number.

$\frac{5}{2} = \underline{\quad}\frac{1}{2}$	$\frac{7}{2} = \underline{\quad}\frac{1}{2}$	$\frac{9}{2} = \underline{\quad}\frac{1}{2}$	$\frac{3}{2} = \underline{\quad}\frac{1}{2}$
$\frac{7}{4} = \underline{\quad}\frac{3}{4}$	$\frac{13}{3} = \underline{\quad}\frac{1}{3}$	$\frac{21}{6} = \underline{\quad}\frac{3}{6}$	$\frac{16}{7} = \underline{\quad}\frac{2}{7}$
$\frac{28}{9} = \underline{\quad}\frac{1}{9}$	$\frac{5}{3} = \underline{\quad}\frac{2}{3}$	$\frac{7}{3} = \underline{\quad}\frac{1}{3}$	$\frac{22}{5} = \underline{\quad}\frac{2}{5}$
$\frac{26}{6} = \underline{\quad}\frac{2}{6}$	$\frac{26}{9} = \underline{\quad}\frac{8}{9}$	$\frac{26}{15} = \underline{\quad}\frac{11}{15}$	$\frac{26}{8} = \underline{\quad}\frac{2}{8}$

Tip!

An improper fraction doubles as a division problem! See what happens when you try to convert the following improper fractions: $^8/_4$, $^{60}/_{10}$, $^{300}/_2$.

Super Sudoku Math: Fractions & Decimals • © 2010 by Eric Charlesworth • Scholastic Teaching Resources

15

Super SUDOKU

Name _____   Date _____

Mixed Review 2
(Simplifying Fractions and Converting Mixed Numbers & Improper Fractions)

Directions

● Every row, column, and 2-by-2 box ⊞ should contain each of these digits:

5   6   7   8

● Fill in each blank with the correct number to solve the problem.

$\frac{3}{24} = \frac{1}{}$	$\frac{15}{2} = \underline{}\frac{1}{2}$	$\frac{15}{18} = \frac{5}{}$	$\frac{11}{55} = \frac{1}{}$
$3\frac{2}{5} = \frac{17}{}$	$\frac{10}{12} = \frac{5}{}$	$1\frac{3}{5} = \frac{}{5}$	$\frac{21}{27} = \frac{}{9}$
$2\frac{1}{3} = \frac{}{3}$	$\frac{9}{24} = \frac{3}{}$	$\frac{17}{3} = \underline{}\frac{2}{3}$	$\frac{12}{22} = \frac{}{11}$
$\frac{33}{5} = \underline{}\frac{3}{5}$	$10\frac{1}{5} = \frac{51}{}$	$\frac{29}{4} = \underline{}\frac{1}{4}$	$\frac{10}{80} = \frac{1}{}$

Before you do any operations with fractions, make sure they are in simplest form. Smaller numbers are easier to work with!

16

Super Sudoku Math: Fractions & Decimals • © 2010 by Eric Charlesworth • Scholastic Teaching Resources

Super SUDOKU

Name _____ Date _____

Adding Fractions

Directions

● Every row, column, and 2-by-2 box ⊞ should contain each of these digits:

$$3 \quad 4 \quad 5 \quad 6$$

● Fill in each blank with the correct number to solve the problem.

$\dfrac{1}{4} + \dfrac{2}{4} = \dfrac{}{4}$	$\dfrac{3}{8} + \dfrac{1}{8} = \dfrac{}{8}$	$\dfrac{1}{4} + \dfrac{3}{8} = \dfrac{}{8}$	$\dfrac{1}{2} + \dfrac{1}{10} = \dfrac{}{10}$
$\dfrac{2}{5} + \dfrac{2}{5} = \dfrac{4}{}$	$\dfrac{1}{6} + \dfrac{2}{3} = \dfrac{5}{}$	$\dfrac{2}{7} + \dfrac{2}{7} = \dfrac{}{7}$	$\dfrac{1}{5} + \dfrac{1}{10} = \dfrac{}{10}$
$\dfrac{1}{3} + \dfrac{2}{12} = \dfrac{}{12}$	$\dfrac{1}{3} + \dfrac{2}{9} = \dfrac{}{9}$	$\dfrac{1}{5} + \dfrac{2}{5} = \dfrac{}{5}$	$\dfrac{1}{5} + \dfrac{1}{15} = \dfrac{}{15}$
$\dfrac{1}{2} + \dfrac{1}{6} = \dfrac{}{6}$	$\dfrac{1}{10} + \dfrac{1}{20} = \dfrac{}{20}$	$\dfrac{2}{4} + \dfrac{2}{8} = \dfrac{}{8}$	$\dfrac{2}{5} + \dfrac{1}{10} = \dfrac{}{10}$

Tip!

To find the lowest common denominator that you need to add or subtract two fractions, find the lowest common multiple of the two denominators.

Name _____ Date _____

Adding Fractions

Directions

● Every row, column, and 2-by-2 box ⊞ should contain each of these digits:

1 2 3 4

● Fill in each blank with the correct number to solve the problem.

● Put your answers in their **simplest form**.

$\dfrac{3}{8} + \dfrac{1}{8} = \dfrac{1}{\rule{0.5em}{0.4pt}}$	$\dfrac{1}{8} + \dfrac{10}{16} = \dfrac{3}{\rule{0.5em}{0.4pt}}$	$\dfrac{1}{6} + \dfrac{1}{6} = \dfrac{\rule{0.5em}{0.4pt}}{3}$	$\dfrac{1}{5} + \dfrac{4}{10} = \dfrac{\rule{0.5em}{0.4pt}}{5}$
$\dfrac{1}{8} + \dfrac{1}{8} = \dfrac{\rule{0.5em}{0.4pt}}{4}$	$\dfrac{8}{30} + \dfrac{2}{5} = \dfrac{2}{\rule{0.5em}{0.4pt}}$	$\dfrac{3}{10} + \dfrac{1}{10} = \dfrac{\rule{0.5em}{0.4pt}}{5}$	$\dfrac{3}{10} + \dfrac{1}{2} = \dfrac{\rule{0.5em}{0.4pt}}{5}$
$\dfrac{1}{9} + \dfrac{1}{3} = \dfrac{\rule{0.5em}{0.4pt}}{9}$	$\dfrac{1}{20} + \dfrac{1}{20} = \dfrac{\rule{0.5em}{0.4pt}}{10}$	$\dfrac{3}{5} + \dfrac{3}{20} = \dfrac{\rule{0.5em}{0.4pt}}{4}$	$\dfrac{1}{2} + \dfrac{1}{6} = \dfrac{\rule{0.5em}{0.4pt}}{3}$
$\dfrac{1}{4} + \dfrac{1}{8} = \dfrac{\rule{0.5em}{0.4pt}}{8}$	$\dfrac{3}{10} + \dfrac{1}{5} = \dfrac{1}{\rule{0.5em}{0.4pt}}$	$\dfrac{30}{50} + \dfrac{4}{20} = \dfrac{\rule{0.5em}{0.4pt}}{5}$	$\dfrac{1}{4} + \dfrac{1}{12} = \dfrac{\rule{0.5em}{0.4pt}}{3}$

Word Problem

Oscar was making cookies. He added ½ cup of white sugar and ⅓ cup of brown sugar. How many total cups of sugar were in the batch of cookies?

_____

Super Sudoku Math: Fractions & Decimals • © 2010 by Eric Charlesworth • Scholastic Teaching Resources

Super SUDOKU

Name _____ Date _____

Subtracting Fractions

Directions

● Every row, column, and 2-by-2 box ⊞ should contain each of these digits:

4   5   6   7

● Fill in each blank with the correct number to solve the problem.

$\dfrac{7}{8} - \dfrac{1}{8} = \dfrac{}{8}$	$\dfrac{6}{7} - \dfrac{2}{7} = \dfrac{}{7}$	$\dfrac{10}{13} - \dfrac{3}{13} = \dfrac{}{13}$	$\dfrac{8}{9} - \dfrac{1}{3} = \dfrac{}{9}$
$\dfrac{8}{9} - \dfrac{1}{9} = \dfrac{}{9}$	$\dfrac{9}{10} - \dfrac{2}{5} = \dfrac{}{10}$	$\dfrac{3}{6} - \dfrac{1}{6} = \dfrac{2}{}$	$\dfrac{3}{4} - \dfrac{2}{4} = \dfrac{1}{}$
$\dfrac{6}{8} - \dfrac{1}{4} = \dfrac{}{8}$	$\dfrac{9}{10} - \dfrac{1}{5} = \dfrac{}{10}$	$\dfrac{2}{3} - \dfrac{1}{4} = \dfrac{}{12}$	$\dfrac{9}{10} - \dfrac{3}{10} = \dfrac{}{10}$
$\dfrac{4}{5} - \dfrac{2}{5} = \dfrac{2}{}$	$\dfrac{1}{2} - \dfrac{1}{3} = \dfrac{1}{}$	$\dfrac{2}{3} - \dfrac{2}{9} = \dfrac{}{9}$	$\dfrac{11}{14} - \dfrac{2}{7} = \dfrac{}{14}$

Word Problem

Jean-Luc went to the deli and got a total of ¾-pound of meats. He bought ⅓-pound of turkey and the rest was roast beef. How much roast beef did he buy?

_____

Super SUDOKU

Name _____ Date _____

Subtracting Fractions

Directions
- Every row, column, and 2-by-2 box ⊞ should contain each of these digits:

1 2 3 4

- Fill in each blank with the correct number to solve the problem.
- Put your answers in their **simplest form**.

$\frac{2}{3} - \frac{5}{12} = \frac{1}{\_}$	$\frac{17}{20} - \frac{1}{4} = \frac{\_}{5}$	$\frac{10}{12} - \frac{1}{6} = \frac{\_}{3}$	$\frac{6}{8} - \frac{1}{4} = \frac{\_}{2}$
$\frac{11}{15} - \frac{1}{3} = \frac{\_}{5}$	$\frac{1}{2} - \frac{2}{5} = \frac{\_}{10}$	$\frac{5}{6} - \frac{1}{12} = \frac{\_}{4}$	$\frac{6}{7} - \frac{2}{7} = \frac{\_}{7}$
$\frac{1}{2} - \frac{1}{5} = \frac{\_}{10}$	$\frac{7}{12} - \frac{1}{3} = \frac{1}{\_}$	$\frac{5}{14} - \frac{3}{14} = \frac{\_}{7}$	$\frac{13}{20} - \frac{1}{4} = \frac{\_}{5}$
$\frac{9}{10} - \frac{7}{10} = \frac{\_}{5}$	$\frac{18}{21} - \frac{4}{7} = \frac{\_}{7}$	$\frac{3}{4} - \frac{1}{2} = \frac{1}{\_}$	$\frac{7}{12} - \frac{1}{4} = \frac{1}{\_}$

Devin has a piece of wood that is $2\frac{11}{12}$ feet long. He wants a piece that is $1\frac{1}{2}$ feet long to help build his skateboard ramp. How much does he need to cut off?

_____

20

Super Sudoku Math: Fractions & Decimals • © 2010 by Eric Charlesworth • Scholastic Teaching Resources

Name _____ Date _____

Mixed Review 3
(Adding and Subtracting Fractions)

Directions

- Every row, column, and 2-by-2 box ⊞ should contain each of these digits:

  1 **2** **3** **4**

- Fill in each blank with the correct number to solve the problem.
- Put your answers in their **simplest form**.

$\frac{1}{8} + \frac{1}{4} = \frac{\quad}{8}$	$\frac{5}{12} + \frac{1}{12} = \frac{\quad}{2}$	$\frac{1}{2} + \frac{1}{4} = \frac{3}{\quad}$	$\frac{1}{9} + \frac{1}{9} = \frac{\quad}{9}$
$\frac{3}{4} - \frac{1}{12} = \frac{\quad}{3}$	$\frac{13}{14} - \frac{5}{14} = \frac{\quad}{7}$	$\frac{7}{12} - \frac{1}{4} = \frac{\quad}{3}$	$\frac{5}{6} - \frac{1}{12} = \frac{\quad}{4}$
$\frac{4}{8} + \frac{1}{4} = \frac{3}{\quad}$	$\frac{1}{3} + \frac{1}{6} = \frac{1}{\quad}$	$\frac{1}{6} + \frac{13}{30} = \frac{\quad}{5}$	$\frac{1}{10} + \frac{1}{10} = \frac{\quad}{5}$
$\frac{5}{6} - \frac{2}{3} = \frac{\quad}{6}$	$\frac{6}{7} - \frac{3}{7} = \frac{\quad}{7}$	$\frac{2}{3} - \frac{4}{15} = \frac{\quad}{5}$	$\frac{8}{9} - \frac{4}{9} = \frac{\quad}{9}$

Word Problem

Kera's club was organizing boxes of used books to donate to the library. Kera brought in a box that was ½ full. Cindy and Chantal each brought boxes that were ¾ full. How many total boxes did they have?

_____

Super SUDOKU

Name _____ Date _____

Multiplying Fractions

Directions

● Every row, column, and 2-by-2 box ⊞ should contain each of these digits:

6 7 8 9

● Fill in each blank with the correct number to solve the problem.

$\frac{1}{2} \times \frac{1}{3} = \frac{1}{\_}$	$\frac{7}{10} \times \frac{1}{4} = \frac{\_}{40}$	$\frac{3}{4} \times \frac{3}{4} = \frac{\_}{16}$	$\frac{4}{5} \times \frac{2}{3} = \frac{\_}{15}$
$\frac{8}{11} \times \frac{1}{3} = \frac{\_}{33}$	$\frac{3}{7} \times \frac{3}{4} = \frac{\_}{28}$	$\frac{1}{2} \times \frac{7}{8} = \frac{\_}{16}$	$\frac{6}{7} \times \frac{1}{3} = \frac{\_}{21}$
$\frac{1}{3} \times \frac{1}{3} = \frac{1}{\_}$	$\frac{2}{3} \times \frac{1}{2} = \frac{2}{\_}$	$\frac{3}{4} \times \frac{1}{2} = \frac{3}{\_}$	$\frac{7}{10} \times \frac{1}{3} = \frac{\_}{30}$
$\frac{3}{1} \times \frac{1}{7} = \frac{3}{\_}$	$\frac{4}{5} \times \frac{2}{5} = \frac{\_}{25}$	$\frac{2}{9} \times \frac{3}{8} = \frac{\_}{72}$	$\frac{2}{3} \times \frac{1}{3} = \frac{2}{\_}$

Word Problem

Randy agreed to mow half of his lawn but then the lawn mower broke when he was only ¾ finished with the job. What fraction of the whole lawn did he mow?

_____

Super Sudoku Math: Fractions & Decimals • © 2010 by Eric Charlesworth • Scholastic Teaching Resources

Name _____ Date _____

Multiplying Fractions

Directions

● Every row, column, and 2-by-2 box ⊞ should contain each of these digits:

6   7   8   9

● Fill in each blank with the correct number to solve the problem.

● Put your answers in their **simplest form**.

$\frac{2}{5} \times \frac{7}{4} = \frac{}{10}$	$\frac{4}{11} \times \frac{3}{2} = \frac{}{11}$	$\frac{7}{2} \times \frac{1}{4} = \frac{7}{}$	$\frac{3}{8} \times \frac{3}{4} = \frac{}{32}$
$\frac{2}{3} \times \frac{7}{6} = \frac{7}{}$	$\frac{3}{2} \times \frac{1}{4} = \frac{3}{}$	$\frac{1}{3} \times \frac{1}{2} = \frac{1}{}$	$\frac{7}{6} \times \frac{1}{2} = \frac{}{12}$
$\frac{3}{6} \times \frac{10}{6} = \frac{5}{}$	$\frac{8}{9} \times \frac{1}{2} = \frac{4}{}$	$\frac{6}{7} \times \frac{1}{2} = \frac{3}{}$	$\frac{4}{6} \times \frac{8}{10} = \frac{}{15}$
$\frac{15}{8} \times \frac{1}{3} = \frac{5}{}$	$\frac{1}{6} \times \frac{6}{7} = \frac{1}{}$	$\frac{2}{3} \times \frac{2}{3} = \frac{4}{}$	$\frac{5}{4} \times \frac{2}{3} = \frac{5}{}$

Word Problem

If you need to multiple a mixed number, convert it to an improper fraction first. For example, try $1\frac{2}{3} \times \frac{1}{5}$.

_____

Super SUDOKU

Name _____ Date _____

Dividing Fractions

Directions

● Every row, column, and 2-by-2 box ⊞ should contain each of these digits:

2 3 4 5

● Fill in each blank with the correct number to solve the problem.

$\dfrac{1}{3} \div \dfrac{1}{2} = \dfrac{}{3}$	$\dfrac{1}{6} \div \dfrac{2}{3} = \dfrac{}{12}$	$\dfrac{1}{8} \div \dfrac{1}{4} = \dfrac{}{8}$	$\dfrac{1}{6} \div \dfrac{1}{5} = \dfrac{}{6}$
$\dfrac{1}{4} \div \dfrac{4}{5} = \dfrac{}{16}$	$\dfrac{2}{5} \div \dfrac{1}{2} = \dfrac{}{5}$	$\dfrac{1}{10} \div \dfrac{1}{2} = \dfrac{}{10}$	$\dfrac{1}{8} \div \dfrac{1}{3} = \dfrac{}{8}$
$\dfrac{1}{4} \div \dfrac{1}{3} = \dfrac{}{4}$	$\dfrac{1}{8} \div \dfrac{1}{2} = \dfrac{}{8}$	$\dfrac{1}{2} \div \dfrac{3}{5} = \dfrac{}{6}$	$\dfrac{2}{7} \div \dfrac{1}{2} = \dfrac{}{7}$
$\dfrac{1}{5} \div \dfrac{3}{4} = \dfrac{}{15}$	$\dfrac{1}{3} \div \dfrac{4}{5} = \dfrac{}{12}$	$\dfrac{1}{5} \div \dfrac{2}{3} = \dfrac{}{10}$	$\dfrac{1}{6} \div \dfrac{1}{2} = \dfrac{}{6}$

Word Problem

Elaine and her two sisters came home and found ¾ of a pizza was left for them. If they split the remaining pizza equally what fraction of a pizza did each sister get?

_____

Super Sudoku Math: Fractions & Decimals • © 2010 by Eric Charlesworth • Scholastic Teaching Resources

Super SUDOKU

Name _____ Date _____

Dividing Fractions

Directions

● Every row, column, and 2-by-2 box ⊞ should contain each of these digits:

6 7 8 9

● Fill in each blank with the correct number to solve the problem.

● Put your answers in their **simplest form**.

$\dfrac{3}{5} \div \dfrac{1}{3} = \dfrac{}{5}$	$\dfrac{6}{7} \div \dfrac{1}{3} = \dfrac{18}{}$	$\dfrac{4}{5} \div \dfrac{1}{2} = \dfrac{}{5}$	$\dfrac{3}{5} \div \dfrac{7}{2} = \dfrac{}{35}$
$\dfrac{1}{4} \div \dfrac{2}{1} = \dfrac{1}{}$	$\dfrac{3}{2} \div \dfrac{7}{4} = \dfrac{}{7}$	$\dfrac{3}{4} \div \dfrac{1}{3} = \dfrac{}{4}$	$\dfrac{10}{21} \div \dfrac{2}{3} = \dfrac{5}{}$
$\dfrac{1}{6} \div \dfrac{1}{7} = \dfrac{7}{}$	$\dfrac{9}{10} \div \dfrac{1}{2} = \dfrac{}{5}$	$\dfrac{5}{14} \div \dfrac{1}{2} = \dfrac{5}{}$	$\dfrac{7}{8} \div \dfrac{1}{5} = \dfrac{35}{}$
$\dfrac{7}{8} \div \dfrac{1}{2} = \dfrac{}{4}$	$\dfrac{8}{10} \div \dfrac{3}{2} = \dfrac{}{15}$	$\dfrac{2}{5} \div \dfrac{1}{3} = \dfrac{}{5}$	$\dfrac{1}{3} \div \dfrac{3}{10} = \dfrac{10}{}$

Tip!

One way to divide a fraction is to make a reciprocal fraction (flip it) and multiply. Another way is to find a common denominator and then divide the numerators.

Name _____ Date _____

Mixed Review 4
(Multiplying & Dividing Fractions)

Directions

- Every row, column, and 2-by-2 box ⊞ should contain each of these digits:

  5   6   7   8

- Fill in each blank with the correct number to solve the problem.
- Put your answers in their **simplest form**.

$\frac{1}{3} \times \frac{2}{4} = \frac{1}{\underline{}}$	$\frac{1}{2} \times \frac{7}{8} = \frac{\underline{}}{16}$	$\frac{1}{4} \times \frac{7}{2} = \frac{7}{\underline{}}$	$\frac{2}{5} \times \frac{1}{2} = \frac{1}{\underline{}}$
$\frac{5}{4} \div \frac{6}{3} = \frac{5}{\underline{}}$	$\frac{2}{5} \div \frac{1}{4} = \frac{8}{\underline{}}$	$\frac{3}{7} \div \frac{1}{2} = \frac{\underline{}}{7}$	$\frac{1}{7} \div \frac{1}{4} = \frac{4}{\underline{}}$
$\frac{5}{6} \times \frac{5}{5} = \frac{\underline{}}{6}$	$\frac{5}{2} \times \frac{5}{3} = \frac{25}{\underline{}}$	$\frac{3}{7} \times \frac{1}{3} = \frac{1}{\underline{}}$	$\frac{5}{2} \times \frac{2}{8} = \frac{5}{\underline{}}$
$\frac{3}{1} \div \frac{7}{2} = \frac{6}{\underline{}}$	$\frac{4}{11} \div \frac{1}{2} = \frac{\underline{}}{11}$	$\frac{4}{1} \div \frac{5}{8} = \frac{32}{\underline{}}$	$\frac{2}{11} \div \frac{1}{3} = \frac{\underline{}}{11}$

Word Problem

Randy came home to find ½ of his birthday cake remaining. He then ate ⅓ of what was on the plate. After he ate, what fraction of the cake was left?

_____

Super Sudoku Math: Fractions & Decimals • © 2010 by Eric Charlesworth • Scholastic Teaching Resources

Super SUDOKU

Name _____ Date _____

Finding the Fraction of a Whole

Directions

● Every row, column, and 2-by-2 box ⊞ should contain each of these digits:

5   6   7   8

● Fill in each blank with the correct number to show the fraction of the whole.

$\frac{1}{2}$ of 10 =	$\frac{2}{3}$ of 9 =	$\frac{1}{3}$ of 21 =	$\frac{4}{5}$ of 10 =
$\frac{1}{}$ of 28 = 4	$\frac{2}{3}$ of 12 =	$\frac{1}{4}$ of 24 =	$\frac{1}{}$ of 100 = 20
$\frac{2}{5}$ of 20 =	$\frac{1}{}$ of 14 = 2	$\frac{1}{4}$ of 20 =	$\frac{3}{10}$ of 20 =
$\frac{}{7}$ of 14 = 12	$\frac{1}{3}$ of 15 =	$\frac{3}{}$ of 40 = 15	$\frac{}{8}$ of 16 = 14

The denominator represents division. So, for example, you can find ½ or ¹⁄₁₀ of a number by dividing that number by 2 or 10. (½ of 30 is 15. ¹⁄₁₀ of 30 is 3.)

Super SUDOKU

Name _____ Date _____

Finding the Fraction of a Whole

Directions

● Every row, column, and 2-by-2 box ⊞ should contain each of these digits:

6   7   8   9

● Fill in each blank with the correct number to show the fraction of the whole.

$\frac{1}{4}$ of __ = 2	$\frac{2}{3}$ of __ = 6	$\frac{1}{2}$ of __ = 3	$\frac{1}{4}$ of 28 =
$\frac{5}{}$ of 36 = 30	$\frac{3}{}$ of 35 = 15	$\frac{7}{}$ of 18 = 14	$\frac{2}{5}$ of 20 =
$\frac{}{10}$ of 100 = 70	$\frac{}{10}$ of 100 = 60	$\frac{3}{4}$ of __ = 6	$\frac{1}{3}$ of 27 =
$\frac{1}{4}$ of 36 =	$\frac{1}{4}$ of 32 =	$\frac{4}{}$ of 70 = 40	$\frac{1}{10}$ of 60 =

Word Problem

Stacey was earning money to buy a 600-dollar computer. After three weeks of working, she said, "I'm already ¾ of the way to my goal!" How much money had Stacey made?

_____

Super Sudoku Math: Fractions & Decimals • © 2010 by Eric Charlesworth • Scholastic Teaching Resources

Name _____ Date _____

Converting Fractions to Decimals

Directions

● Every row, column, and 2-by-2 box ⊞ should contain each of these digits:

1   **2**   **3**   **4**

● Fill in each blank with the correct number to convert the fraction to a decimal.

$\frac{1}{10} = 0.\underline{}$	$\frac{1}{5} = 0.\underline{}$	$\frac{2}{} = 0.5$	$\frac{}{6} = 0.5$
$\frac{3}{10} = 0.\underline{}$	$\frac{2}{5} = 0.\underline{}$	$\frac{}{10} = 0.2$	$\frac{}{2} = 0.5$
$\frac{2}{10} = 0.\underline{}$	$\frac{2}{20} = 0.\underline{}$	$\frac{}{10} = 0.3$	$\frac{}{10} = 0.4$
$\frac{4}{10} = 0.\underline{}$	$\frac{6}{20} = 0.\underline{}$	$\frac{}{10} = 0.1$	$\frac{4}{20} = 0.\underline{}$

Tip!

Decimals are just fractions written in a different way. And decimals always have denominators that are powers of 10 (10, 100, 1,000, etc.).

Name _____ Date _____

Converting Fractions to Decimals

Directions

● Every row, column, and 2-by-2 box ⊞ should contain each of these digits:

$$5 \quad 6 \quad 7 \quad 8$$

● Fill in each blank with the correct number to convert the fraction to a decimal.

$\frac{1}{2} = 0.\underline{}$	$\frac{40}{50} = 0.\underline{}$	$\frac{37}{100} = 0.3\underline{}$	$\frac{31}{50} = 0.\underline{}2$
$\frac{12}{20} = 0.\underline{}$	$\frac{14}{20} = 0.\underline{}$	$\frac{2}{25} = 0.0\underline{}$	$\frac{20}{40} = 0.\underline{}$
$\frac{20}{25} = 0.\underline{}$	$\frac{1}{4} = 0.2\underline{}$	$\frac{60}{100} = 0.\underline{}$	$\frac{35}{50} = 0.\underline{}$
$\frac{17}{100} = 0.1\underline{}$	$\frac{9}{15} = 0.\underline{}$	$\frac{3}{4} = 0.7\underline{}$	$\frac{32}{40} = 0.\underline{}$

Tip!

Another way to convert fractions to decimals is to simply do the division. To change ¼ to a decimal, divide 1 by 4. Play around with fractions using a calculator and you'll find lots of interesting patterns!

Super Sudoku Math: Fractions & Decimals • © 2010 by Eric Charlesworth • Scholastic Teaching Resources

Name _____ Date _____

Mixed Review 5
(Finding the Fraction of a Whole and Converting Fractions to Decimals)

Directions

● Every row, column, and 2-by-2 box ⊞ should contain each of these digits:

3 4 5 6

● Fill in each blank with the correct number to solve the problem.

$\frac{1}{3}$ of 12 =	$\frac{1}{5}$ of 25 =	$\frac{2}{3}$ of 9 =	$\frac{1}{10}$ of 30 =
$\frac{6}{20}$ = 0.__	$\frac{3}{5}$ = 0.__	$\frac{2}{5}$ = 0.__	$\frac{1}{2}$ = 0.__
$\frac{1}{2}$ of 10 =	$\frac{2}{3}$ of 6 =	$\frac{3}{4}$ of 40 = __0	$\frac{1}{2}$ of 32 = 1__
$\frac{16}{100}$ = 0.1__	$\frac{23}{100}$ = 0.2__	$\frac{40}{80}$ = 0.__	$\frac{40}{100}$ = 0.__

Word Problem

Juan and Allie worked together to collect 200 beach stones. After they were done, Allie kept ⅘ of the stones. How many did each of them keep?

_____

Super SUDOKU

Name _____ Date _____

Adding Decimals

Directions

● Every row, column, and 2-by-2 box ⊞ should contain each of these digits:

6   7   8   9

● Fill in each blank with the correct number to solve the problem.

0.3 + 0.5 ——— 0.__	0.15 + 0.45 ——— 0.__	0.6 + 0.3 ——— 0.__	0.4 + 0.3 ——— 0.__
0.33 + 0.57 ——— 0.__	0.14 + 0.56 ——— 0.__	0.6 + 0.2 ——— 0.__	0.3 + 0.3 ——— 0.__
0.51 + 0.09 ——— 0.__	0.85 + 0.05 ——— 0.__	0.32 + 0.42 ——— 0.__4	0.04 + 0.04 ——— 0.0__
0.25 + 0.5 ——— 0.__5	0.02 + 0.8 ——— 0.__2	0.5 + 0.1 ——— 0.__	0.2 + 0.7 ——— 0.__

Word Problem

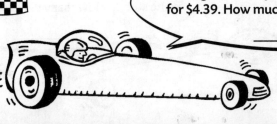

Alex bought a hockey stick for $25.70 and a puck for $4.39. How much did he spend in total?

_____

Super Sudoku Math: Fractions & Decimals • © 2010 by Eric Charlesworth • Scholastic Teaching Resources

Super SUDOKU

Name _____ Date _____

Adding Decimals

Directions

● Every row, column, and 2-by-2 box ⊞ should contain each of these digits:

1 **2** **3** **4**

● Fill in each blank with the correct number to solve the problem.

2.6 9 + 3.8 ――― 6._ 9	7.9 + 0.45 ――― 8._5	3.22 + 5 ――― 8.2_	7.9 + 1.2 ――― 9._
2.11 + 3.2 ――― 5.3_	0.4 + 0.92 ――― 1.3_	2.12 + 4.3 ――― 6._2	1.5 + 1.5 ――― _.0
1.7 + 1.63 ――― 3.3_	2.9 + 1.2 ――― _.1	2.456 + 0.7 ――― 3._56	0.6 + 0.6 ――― 1._
1.5 + 0.5 ――― _.0	0.6 + 0.45 ――― _.05	7.4 + 0.95 ――― 8._5	0.33 + 3.9 ――― _.23

Tip!

When adding decimals with different place values, start by lining up the decimal points vertically. (To help you keep track of the place values, you can add place-holder zeros.) Then add the usual way. Remember to line up the decimal points in your answer.

Super SUDOKU

Name _____ Date _____

Subtracting Decimals

Directions

● Every row, column, and 2-by-2 box ⊞ should contain each of these digits:

1 **2** **3** **4**

● Fill in each blank with the correct number to solve the problem.

0.2 − 0.1 ――― 0.__	0.42 − 0.22 ――― 0.__	0.84 − 0.81 ――― 0.0__	0.74 − 0.7 ――― 0.0__
0.8 − 0.5 ――― 0.__	0.7 − 0.3 ――― 0.__	0.95 − 0.75 ――― 0.__	0.43 − 0.22 ――― 0.2__
0.81 − 0.4 ――― 0.__1	0.9 − 0.6 ――― 0.__	0.7 − 0.6 ――― 0.__	0.39 − 0.1 ――― 0.__9
0.49 − 0.26 ――― 0.__3	0.08 − 0.07 ――― 0.0__	0.98 − 0.84 ――― 0.1__	0.3 − 0.27 ――― 0.0__

Word Problem

Packs of extra long-lasting gum are on sale for $0.45 each. Annie has two dollars. How many packs can she buy and how much money will she have left?

_____

34

Super Sudoku Math: Fractions & Decimals • © 2010 by Eric Charlesworth • Scholastic Teaching Resources

Super SUDOKU

Name _____ Date _____

Subtracting Decimals

Directions

● Every row, column, and 2-by-2 box ⊞ should contain each of these digits:

1   2   3   4

● Fill in each blank with the correct number to solve the problem.

3.46 − 1.8 ___.66	2.95 − 1.6 1.__5	4.29 − 1.27 3.0__	3.6 − 1.12 2.__8
4 − 2.8 1.__	4 − 2.6 1.__	4 − 2.7 1.__	4 − 2.9 1.__
8.6 − 5.49 ___.11	3.41 − 3.2 0.2__	5.72 − 1 ___.72	10 − 8.68 1.3__
8.4 − 7 1.__	9.2 − 6 3.__	4 − 3.29 0.7__	1 − 0.7 0.__

Word Problem

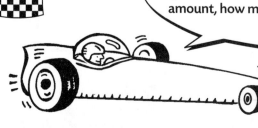
Greg had 1.7 pounds of grapes before he gave ¼ of a pound to his friend Suzanne. After he gave away that amount, how many pounds of grapes did he have left?

_____

Super SUDOKU

Name _____ Date _____

Mixed Review 6
(Adding and Subtracting Decimals)

Directions

● Every row, column, and 2-by-2 box ⊞ should contain each of these digits:

6 7 8 9

● Fill in each blank with the correct number to solve the problem.

0.26 − 0.2 ―――― 0.0_	1.1 − 0.3 ―――― 0._	3.4 − 1.5 ―――― 1._	1.3 − 1.23 ―――― 0.0_
0.43 + 0.3 ―――― 0._3	1.4 + 2.5 ―――― 3._	3.1 + 3.1 ―――― _.2	4. 92 + 4 ―――― _.92
2.2 − 1.4 ―――― 0._	2.1 − 0.5 ―――― 1._	2.1 − 0.35 ―――― 1._5	2.8 − 0.9 ―――― 1._
0.3 + 0.6 ―――― 0._	6 + 1.1 ―――― _.1	0.6 + 0.88 ―――― 1.4_	3.6 + 3.3 ―――― _.9

Word Problem

If Alexa has a coupon that allows her five dollars off any purchase and she buys four books that cost $9.35 each, how much will she be charged?

_____

Super Sudoku Math: Fractions & Decimals • © 2010 by Eric Charlesworth • Scholastic Teaching Resources

Super SUDOKU

Name _____ Date _____

Multiplying Decimals

Directions

● Every row, column, and 2-by-2 box ⊞ should contain each of these digits:

1   2   3   4

● Fill in each blank with the correct number to solve the problem.

0.5 × 2 ___.0	0.5 × 4 ___.0	0.8 × 6 ___.8	0.9 × 0.4 0.___6
3 × 0.1 0.___	4 × 0.1 0.___	0.8 × 0.3 0.___4	0.9 × 2 ___.8
0.7 × 0.6 0.___2	0.2 × 8 ___.6	1.1 × 3 3.___	4.1 × 2 8.___
0.5 × 0.5 0.___5	0.6 × 5 ___.0	3 × 0.4 ___.2	8 × 0.5 ___.0

Word Problem

Lorri is baking 2.5 batches of brownies.
She needs 1.5 cups of flour for each batch.
How many cups of flower does she need in all?

_____

Super SUDOKU

Name _____ Date _____

Multiplying Decimals

Directions

● Every row, column, and 2-by-2 box ⊞ should contain each of these digits:

1   2   3   4

● Fill in each blank with the correct number to solve the problem.

2.2 × 1.6 ——— __.52	5 × 0.8 ——— __.0	7.2 × 1.4 ——— __0.08	0.22 × 11 ——— 2.4__
0.18 × 0.7 ——— 0.__26	20 × 1.6 ——— 3__	13 × 0.68 ——— 8.8__	0.9 × 0.7 ——— 0.6__
1.3 × 0.4 ——— 0.5__	0.81 × 0.1 ——— 0.08__	15 × 0.2 ——— __.0	2.1 × 2.1 ——— 4.__1
30 × 0.8 ——— 2__.0	5.1 × 1.3 ——— 6.6__	3.1 × 2 ——— 6.__	1.4 × 1.4 ——— __.96

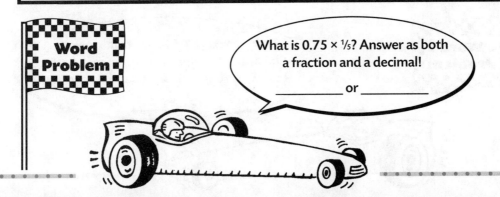

Word Problem

What is 0.75 × ⅕? Answer as both a fraction and a decimal!

_____ or _____

Super Sudoku Math: Fractions & Decimals • © 2010 by Eric Charlesworth • Scholastic Teaching Resources

Super SUDOKU

Name _____ Date _____

Dividing Decimals

Directions

● Every row, column, and 2-by-2 box ⊞ should contain each of these digits:

2   3   4   5

● Fill in each blank with the correct number to solve the problem.

$0.3\overline{)0.6}$	$0.3\overline{)1.2}$	$0.4\overline{)2}$	$1.2\overline{)3.6}$
$0.2\overline{)1}$	$0.8\overline{)2.4}$	$0.8\overline{)1.6}$	$1.2\overline{)4.8}$
$0.2\overline{)0.8}$	$1.2\overline{)6}$	$2.8\overline{)8.4}$	$2.3\overline{)4.6}$
$0.3\overline{)0.9}$	$1.4\overline{)2.8}$	$2.5\overline{)10}$	$2.5\overline{)12.5}$

Word Problem

Sean had 100 ounces of juice and was dividing it up into glasses that held 12.5 ounces each. How many glasses did he pour?

_____

Super SUDOKU

Name _____ Date _____

Dividing Decimals

Directions

● Every row, column, and 2-by-2 box ⊞ should contain each of these digits:

5   6   7   8

● Fill in each blank with the correct number to solve the problem.

$0.6\overline{)3.6}$	$2.4\overline{)12}$	$1.1\overline{)7.7}$	$5.2\overline{)41.6}$
$0.2\overline{)1.6}$	$1.5\overline{)10.5}$	$4.2\overline{)21}$	$1.02\overline{)6.12}$
$11.6\overline{)58}$	$0.07\overline{)0.56}$	$0.07\overline{)0.42}$	$1.8\overline{)12.6}$
$0.81\overline{)5.67}$	$0.4\overline{)2.4}$	$0.9\overline{)7.2}$	$9.9\overline{)49.5}$

Word Problem

Sarafina has ten dollars. She wants to buy a notebook and two folders for each school subject. If a notebook costs $2.29 and a folder costs $0.40, how many sets can she buy?

_____

Super Sudoku Math: Fractions & Decimals • © 2010 by Eric Charlesworth • Scholastic Teaching Resources

Super SUDOKU

Name _____ Date _____

Mixed Review 7
(Multiplying and Dividing Decimals)

Directions

● Every row, column, and 2-by-2 box ⊞ should contain each of these digits:

1   2   3   4

● Fill in each blank with the correct number to solve the problem.

3.1 × 0.5 ___.55	0.6 × 2 1.__	1.1 × 4 4.__	0.7 × 0.9 0.6__
0.9)‾2.7	0.9)‾3.6	2.7)‾5.4	8.2)‾8.2
0.7 × 0.6 0.__2	3 × 0.4 __.2	3 × 1.2 __.6	0.4 × 0.5 0.__0
5.1)‾10.2	1.3)‾3.9	0.4)‾0.4	.08)‾0.32

Word Problem

Four identical statues were shipped in a box that weighed 9.6 kilograms. How much did each statue weigh?

_____

Name _____ Date _____

Converting Fractions to Percents

Directions

● Every row, column, and 2-by-2 box ⊞ should contain each of these digits:

3   4   5   6

● Fill in each blank with the correct number to convert the fractions to percents.

$\dfrac{2}{5} = \_0\%$	$\dfrac{6}{10} = \_0\%$	$\dfrac{1}{2} = \_0\%$	$\dfrac{6}{20} = \_0\%$
$\dfrac{1}{4} = 2\_\%$	$\dfrac{9}{30} = \_0\%$	$\dfrac{8}{20} = \_0\%$	$\dfrac{3}{5} = \_0\%$
$\dfrac{12}{20} = \_0\%$	$\dfrac{35}{100} = 3\_\%$	$\dfrac{53}{100} = 5\_\%$	$\dfrac{7}{50} = 1\_\%$
$\dfrac{3}{10} = \_0\%$	$\dfrac{11}{25} = 4\_\%$	$\dfrac{36}{100} = 3\_\%$	$\dfrac{5}{100} = \_\%$

Percents, like decimals, are a way to write fractions. In fact, writing percents is the same as writing a decimal to the hundredths place (you multiply the decimal by 100).

Super Sudoku Math: Fractions & Decimals • © 2010 by Eric Charlesworth • Scholastic Teaching Resources

Name _____ Date _____

Converting Fractions to Percents

Directions

● Every row, column, and 2-by-2 box ⊞ should contain each of these digits:

1   2   3   4

● Fill in each blank with the correct number to convert the fractions to percents.

$\frac{2}{10}$ = __0%	$\frac{4}{10}$ = __0%	$\frac{1}{10}$ = __0%	$\frac{3}{10}$ = __0%
$\frac{5}{5}$ = __00%	$\frac{23}{100}$ = 2__%	$\frac{21}{50}$ = 4__%	$\frac{42}{100}$ = __2%
$\frac{64}{100}$ = 6__%	$\frac{21}{100}$ = 2__%	$\frac{73}{100}$ = 7__%	$\frac{27}{100}$ = __7%
$\frac{93}{100}$ = 9__%	$\frac{13}{25}$ = 5__%	$\frac{49}{100}$ = __9%	$\frac{4}{25}$ = __6%

Word Problem

On her fractions conversion test, Corey got 17 out of 20 questions correct. What was her score as a percent?

_____

Super SUDOKU

Name _____ Date _____

Finding the Percent of a Whole

Directions

● Every row, column, and 2-by-2 box ⊞ should contain each of these digits:

| 5 | 6 | 7 | 8 |

● Fill in each blank with the correct number to show the percent of the whole number.

100% of 8 =	100% of 6 =	100% of 5 =	100% of 7 =
50% of 10 =	50% of 14 =	50% of 16 =	50% of 12 =
25% of 24 =	25% of 20 =	25% of 28 =	25% of 32 =
10% of 70 =	10% of 80 =	10% of 60 =	10% of 50 =

Word Problem

In a class election, Alec received 60% of the vote. If a total of 300 students voted, how many of them voted for Alec?

_____

Super Sudoku Math: Fractions & Decimals • © 2010 by Eric Charlesworth • Scholastic Teaching Resources

Super SUDOKU

Name _____ Date _____

Finding the Percent of a Whole

Directions

● Every row, column, and 2-by-2 box  should contain each of these digits:

2   3   4   5

● Fill in each blank with the correct number to show the percent of the whole number.

50% of 4 =	50% of 8 =	50% of 10 =	50% of 6 =
25% of 20 =	25% of 12 =	25% of 8 =	25% of 16 =
10% of 40 =	10% of 50 =	10% of 30 =	10% of 20 =
5% of 60 =	5% of 40 =	5% of 80 =	5% of 100 =

Word Problem

Frank's pool can hold 2,000 gallons of water and it is 75% full. How many more gallons does Frank need to put in to fill it up?

_____

Name _____   Date _____

Mixed Review 8
(Converting Fractions to Percents and Finding the Percent of a Whole)

Directions

● Every row, column, and 2-by-2 box ⊞ should contain each of these digits:

6   7   8   9

● Fill in each blank with the correct number to solve the problem.

$\frac{3}{5}$ = __0%	$\frac{7}{10}$ = __0%	$\frac{45}{50}$ = __0%	$\frac{4}{5}$ = __0%
50% of 16 =	25% of 36 =	50% of 14 =	30% of 20 =
$\frac{67}{100}$ = 6__%	$\frac{82}{100}$ = __2%	$\frac{64}{100}$ = __4%	$\frac{91}{100}$ = __1%
50% of 18 =	6% of 100 =	40% of 20 =	20% of 35 =

Word Problem

In May, Ann earned 108 dollars babysitting. After she used 25% of her earnings to buy a concert ticket, how much did she have left?

_____

Super Sudoku Math: Fractions & Decimals • © 2010 by Eric Charlesworth • Scholastic Teaching Resources

Super SUDOKU

Name _____ Date _____

Final Mixed Review

Directions

● Every row, column, and 2-by-2 box ⊞ should contain each of these digits:

6 7 8 9

● Fill in each blank with the correct number to solve the problem.
● Put your answers in their **simplest form**.

$\square = \dfrac{1}{\underline{}}$	$\dfrac{14}{18} = \dfrac{7}{\underline{}}$	$\dfrac{3}{21} = \dfrac{1}{\underline{}}$	$2\dfrac{2}{3} = \dfrac{\underline{}}{3}$
$\dfrac{1}{5}$ of 35 =	$\dfrac{2}{5}$ of 20 =	$\dfrac{9}{7} \div \dfrac{3}{2} = \dfrac{\underline{}}{7}$	$\dfrac{7}{10} - \dfrac{1}{4} = \dfrac{\underline{}}{20}$
$\dfrac{2}{3} \times \dfrac{3}{9} = \dfrac{2}{\underline{}}$	$\dfrac{28}{40} = 0.\underline{}$	$\begin{array}{r} 1.8 \\ +\,4 \\ \hline 5.\underline{} \end{array}$	$\begin{array}{r} 2.1 \\ -\,0.5 \\ \hline 1.\underline{} \end{array}$
$\begin{array}{r} 2.5 \\ \times\ 3.2 \\ \hline \underline{}.00 \end{array}$	$0.6\overline{)3.6}$	$\dfrac{18}{20} = \underline{}0\%$	50% of 14 =

Word Problem

This one's tough, but you can do it!
What is ⅓ of 50% of ⅔ of 20% of 45?

_____

Super Sudoku Math: Fractions & Decimals • © 2010 by Eric Charlesworth • Scholastic Teaching Resources

47

Answer Key

Page 7

3	1	4	2
2	4	1	3
4	2	3	1
1	3	2	4

Page 8

6	7	5	4
4	5	7	6
5	4	6	7
7	6	4	5

Page 9

1	4	3	2
2	3	4	1
4	1	2	3
3	2	1	4

Page 10

7	8	9	6
6	9	7	8
8	7	6	9
9	6	8	7

Word Problem: Many possible answers including $\frac{10}{15}$, $\frac{2}{3}$, and $\frac{4}{6}$.

Page 11

4	2	3	1
3	1	4	2
1	4	2	3
2	3	1	4

Page 12

2	3	4	1
1	4	2	3
3	2	1	4
4	1	3	2

Page 13

4	6	7	5
5	7	4	6
6	4	5	7
7	5	6	4

Word Problem: They can both play the same number of songs: $\frac{2}{3} = \frac{4}{6}$.

Page 14

9	7	8	6
6	8	9	7
8	6	7	9
7	9	6	8

Page 15

2	3	4	1
1	4	3	2
3	1	2	4
4	2	1	3

Page 16

8	7	6	5
5	6	8	7
7	8	5	6
6	5	7	8

Page 17

3	4	5	6
5	6	4	3
6	5	3	4
4	3	6	5

Page 18

2	4	1	3
1	3	2	4
4	1	3	2
3	2	4	1

Word Problem: $\frac{5}{6}$ cup

Page 19

6	4	7	5
7	5	6	4
4	7	5	6
5	6	4	7

Word Problem: $\frac{5}{12}$ pound

Page 20

4	3	2	1
2	1	3	4
3	4	1	2
1	2	4	3

Word Problem: $1\frac{5}{12}$ feet

Page 21

3	1	4	2
2	4	1	3
4	2	3	1
1	3	2	4

Word Problem: 2 boxes

Page 22

6	7	9	8
8	9	7	6
9	6	8	7
7	8	6	9

Word Problem: $\frac{3}{8}$

Page 23

7	6	8	9
9	8	6	7
6	9	7	8
8	7	9	6

Word Problem: $\frac{5}{15}$ or $\frac{1}{3}$

Page 24

2	3	4	5
5	4	2	3
3	2	5	4
4	5	3	2

Word Problem: $\frac{1}{4}$ of a pizza

Page 25

9	7	8	6
8	6	9	7
6	9	7	8
7	8	6	9

Page 26

6	7	8	5
8	5	6	7
5	6	7	8
7	8	5	6

Word Problem: $\frac{2}{6}$ or $\frac{1}{3}$